W9-BNU-794

BUG

IN A

RUG

Joanna Cole *and* **Stephanie Calmenson**

BUG IN A RUG

READING FUN
FOR JUST-BEGINNERS

Illustrated by **Alan Tiegreen**

Morrow Junior Books
New York

To "just-beginners" everywhere
—J.C. and S.C.

Text copyright © 1996 by Joanna Cole and Stephanie Calmenson
Illustrations copyright © 1996 by Alan Tiegreen

All rights reserved. No part of this book may be reproduced or
utilized in any form or by any means, electronic or mechanical,
including photocopying, recording, or by any information storage
and retrieval system, without permission in writing from the Publisher.
Inquiries should be addressed to William Morrow and Company, Inc.,
1350 Avenue of the Americas, New York, NY 10019.

Printed in the United States of America.

10 9 8 7 6 5 4 3 2 1

Library of Congress Cataloging-in-Publication Data
Cole, Joanna.
Bug in a rug / by Joanna Cole and Stephanie Calmenson;
illustrated by Alan Tiegreen.
p. cm.
Summary: Includes simple stories and poems, labeled pictures,
and rebuses to help young children discover the pleasure of reading.
ISBN 0-688-12208-6 (trade)—ISBN 0-688-12209-4 (library)
1. Children's literature, American. [1. Literature—Collections. 2. Alphabet.]
I. Calmenson, Stephanie. II. Tiegreen, Alan, ill. III. Title.
PZ5.C7172Bu 1996 [E]—dc20 95-35355 CIP AC

Reading Bug
In a rug,
Would you like
A great big hug?

CONTENTS

HELPING CHILDREN READ
A NOTE TO PARENTS AND TEACHERS

One of the most exciting moments in a child's life is when that child first reads independently. Of course, learning to read does not happen in a single moment. It is a process that takes place over time. And it does not happen because of one book, one reading series, or even one person. There are many roads to reading. And there are many ways you can help. You've probably already begun.

You cannot do any better for your child than to read aloud together. Books will make your child laugh. They will give you a chance to cuddle together. They will answer your child's questions. Laughter, cuddling, solving life's mysteries. What child wouldn't want to read?

The key to reading with young children is to have fun without pressure and without formal teaching. Along with story time, your child may also enjoy simple reading activities, such as finding the first letter of his name in signs, pretending to read his favorite books, and pretending to write stories, letters, and messages. These are no-pressure activities that allow your child to succeed. The book you are holding offers other reading activities to enjoy.

This is a book for parents, teachers, and children to share. It's a book to relax and have fun with. Depending on your child's level of skills, you will read more or less of the book aloud, with children joining in by naming pictures, identifying letters and sounds, telling stories in their own words, and, when they are ready, reading simple words.

We have tried to make the book as inviting as possible, while offering five categories of skills that help children learn. We begin with activities that introduce the letters. At first, learning the alphabet in order is not as important as becoming familiar with each letter and the sounds it makes.

A section of activities with picture clues and labels helps children realize that printed words stand for objects they already know in their world. With rebus stories, in which the parent reads the words and the child "reads" the pictures, the child learns firsthand that in English reading goes from left to right and that each printed word or picture stands for a spoken word.

We include interactive poems, chants, and a song because young children can never have too much rhyming. Reading specialists have learned that, in general, pre-reading children who are familiar with rhyming words will learn to read better and more easily later on.

At the very end, we offer a selection of "mini-books" within the book. After hearing these stories a few times, young children may try reading or telling these very simple tales on their own. Such success is a great enticement to learning.

Indeed, it is more important for pre-readers to experience success and pleasure with books than to master skills. Perhaps your child cannot yet decipher the word *bear*, but she knows it starts with *b* and, after you read it aloud, she can say the word herself. Another preschooler may not know the letters yet, but he can "read" pictures in a rebus; after listening to a parent read a word, he can find the picture that goes with it; he can guess what will happen next in a mini-story. In short, he can experience success.

Joanna Cole and Stephanie Calmenson

LETTER PARADE

Some letters of the alphabet rhyme.
Listen to this poem and you will hear them.

Hello, *A*.
Where is *B*?
Walking with the letter *C*.
Here comes *D* with the letter *E*.
Right behind them are *F* and *G*.
Hello, *H*, *I*, and *J*.
"Wait up!" calls the letter *K*.
L, *M*, *N*, *O*, and *P*
Race ahead so they can see.
Q, *R*, *S*, *T*, *U*, and *V*
March with *W*, *X*, *Y*, and *Z*.

Wait up!

11

ALPHABET SOUP

Name the pictures or read the words.
You'll find one for every letter of the alphabet.

apple bug cup dog egg fan girl

oar pig queen rug sun tree

Wait up!

ALPHABET SOUP

Name the pictures or read the words.
You'll find one for every letter of the alphabet.

apple   bug   cup   dog   egg   fan   girl

a
b
c
d
e
f
g
h
i
j
k
l
m
n
o
p
q
r
s
t
u
v
w
x
y
z

oar   pig   queen   rug   sun   tree

hat ice jar kite lamp moon nest

umbrella violin web X ray yo-yo zebra

ON THE ROAD

Do you know the sound b makes?
Can you find the things that begin with b?
Do the same thing with the letter p.

POLICE

POST OFFICE

BAKERY

PUMPKINS

Next time you
are on the road,
try this game
with any letters.

15

ME

Can you read the words on these pages?
Let the pictures help you.

HAT

EYE

HAIR

EAR

SHIRT

ELBOW

HAND

SHORTS

FEELER

WING

BODY

LEG

NOSE

MOUTH

NECK

ARM

STOMACH

FINGER

LEG

TOE

KNEE

FOOT

SOCK

SHOE

16

MY ROOM

RUN, DOG, RUN!

In each picture, one thing changes.
Can you see how? Can you read about it?

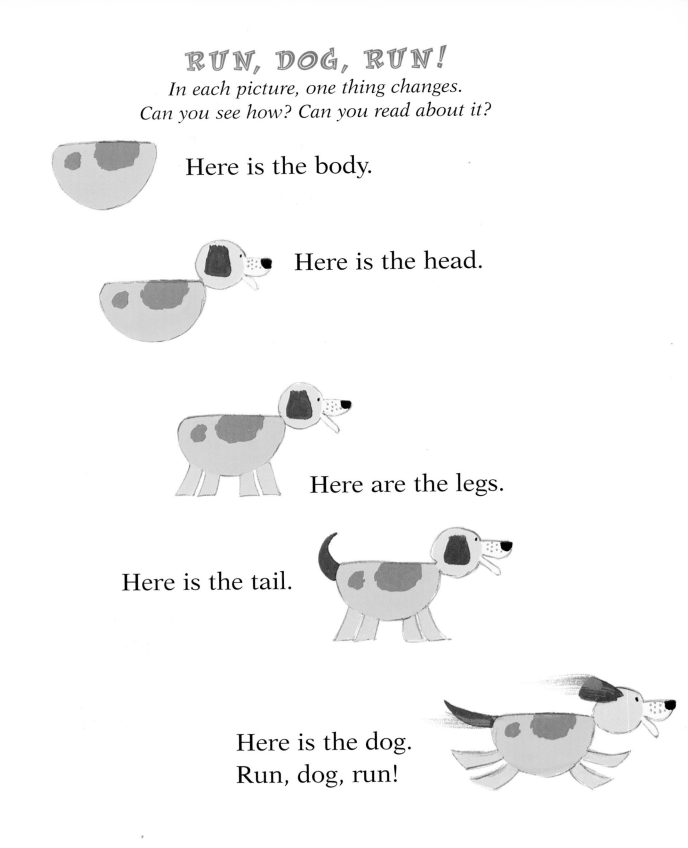

Here is the body.

Here is the head.

Here are the legs.

Here is the tail.

Here is the dog.
Run, dog, run!

Here is the body.

Here is the cab.

Here are the wheels.

Here is the driver.

Here is the truck.
Go, truck, go!

WAGMOR
DOG
FOOD

WHAT THE CROOK TOOK

Listen to the poem. Look at the picture on this page.
Can you find what the crook took?

There is a crook in this book.
Do you know what he took?
Take a look:
A hat. A mat.
A coat. A boat.
A bear. A chair.

WHAT THE CROOK GAVE BACK

Look at the picture on this page.
Can you find the gifts the crook left?

The crook is sad.
He feels bad.
He opens his pack.
He gives everything back.
"Look," says the crook.
"Six things are new.
I left them here as gifts for you:
A rock. A clock.
A mouse. A house.
A cup. A pup."

I AM COLD!

You can read this poem together.
Parents read the words. Kids read the pictures.

A  got my 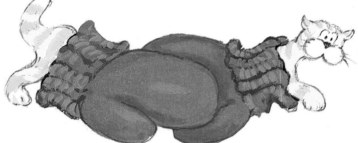 .

Her ![cats] got my ![mittens] .

Some ![kangaroos] got my ![shoes] .

22

A  got my .

A got my .

Brrrr! I am cold!

23

BUG IN A RUG

Can you help read this picture story?

has a ⬜ .

has a 📕 .

wants to read. Where will go?

sees a 🪑 . The 🪑 is too hard.

sees a 🛏️ .

The  is too big.

sees a .

The is not too hard.

The is not too big.

is snug in the .

25

THE CLOWN AND THE ELEPHANT

Here is another picture story to read together.

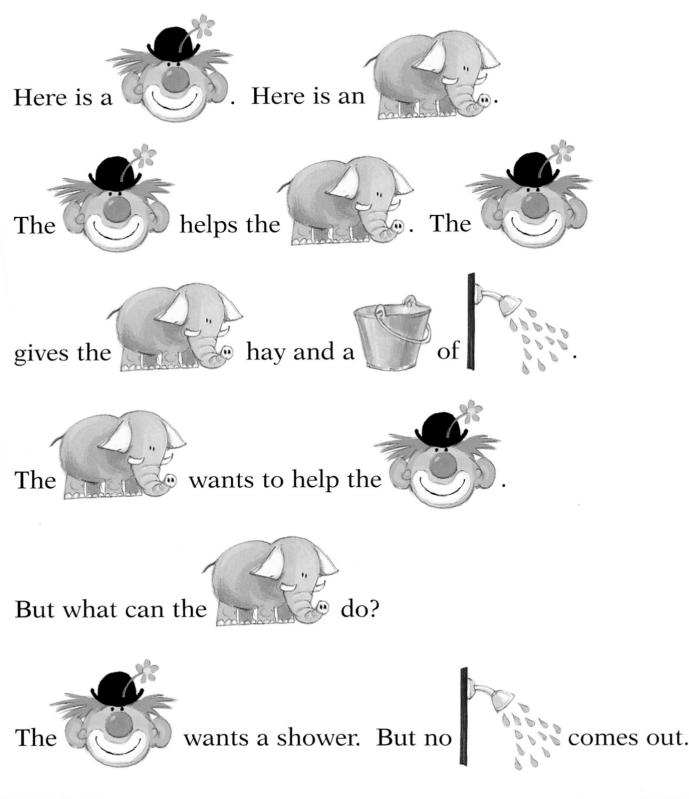

Here is a 🤡. Here is an 🐘.

The 🤡 helps the 🐘. The 🤡

gives the 🐘 hay and a 🪣 of 🚿.

The 🐘 wants to help the 🤡.

But what can the 🐘 do?

The 🤡 wants a shower. But no 🚿 comes out.

Now the  helps the . The puts

his into the and gives the a shower.

"Thank you, dear ," says the .

27

I LOVE SPAGHETTI!

Now you are good at reading picture stories. How about a long one?

[dog] sent a [letter] to [rabbit] . [dog] sent

a [letter] to [frog] . He sent a [letter] to [cat] .

The [letter] said, "Come to my [doghouse] for dinner. Please bring

your favorite food. Love, [dog] ." [rabbit] got the [letter] .

"What will I bring?" thought [rabbit] . "I like [carrots] .

But I *love* [spaghetti] ." So [rabbit] made [spaghetti] .

[frog] got the [letter] . "What will I bring?" thought [frog] .

"I like [flies] . But I *love* [spaghetti] ."

So [frog] made [spaghetti]. [tiger] got the [note].

"What will I bring?" thought [tiger]. "I like [mice].

But I *love* [spaghetti]." So [tiger] made [spaghetti].

[dog]'s friends went to his [doghouse]. They each had a [pot].

[dog] had a [pot], too. What did he make?

He made [spaghetti]! Because everyone loves [spaghetti]!

HOW WE GO

This poem is a name game.
Read it and see.

Mike

bike

Gus

bus

SCHOOL BUS

Jane

plane

dragon

wagon

Nan

van

Can you make rhymes with your name?

THINGS TO DO TODAY

This list is a poem. Each line has a rhyme.

Hug a bug.

Pat a cat.

Jog with a frog.

Leap with a sheep.

Play house with a mouse.

Make a wish with a fish.

Be funny with a bunny.

Wave good-bye to a fly.

Can you think of other things to do?
Can you make them rhyme?

WHERE IS BEAR?

Some rhyming words are missing in this poem.
Do you know what they are? Use the pictures to help.

Where is the key? It is on the  .

Where is Bear's hat? It is on his .

Where is Bear's sock? It is under the .

Where is Bear's shoe? It is in the .

Where is Bear? He is in a eating a !

WHO DOES IT?

Who goes fast? Who goes slow?
Name the animal if you know.

Who goes fast?
Who goes slow?

Who lives in sand?
Who lives in snow?

Who flies in the air?
Who swims in the sea?

Who spins a web?
Who hangs from a tree?

Who plays with yarn?
Who chews a shoe?

Who finished this page?
Could it be you?

DO YOU WANT TO BE A BEE?

Sing this as a song. Or say it as a poem.
Either way, make it noisy!

Do you want to be a bee and *buzz*?
Do you want to be a cow and *moo*?
Do you want to be a duck and *quack*?
Do you want to be something new?

Yes, I want to be a bee and *buzz*.
Yes, I want to be a cow and *moo*.
Yes, I want to be a duck and *quack*.
Yes, I want to be something new!

Buzz!

Moo!

Quack, quack!

Woof!

What else do you want to be?
Can you sing about it?

MINE!

A One-Word Story
Mine *is the only word in this story.*
It's fun to read this story. It's fun to tell it in your own words, too!

Mine.

Mine.

Mine.

MINE!

NO! YES!
A Two-Word Story

No!

No!

No!

Yes! Yes! Yes!

BIG PIG WIG
A Three-Word Story

Pig.

Wig.

Big pig.

Wig!

Wig.

Big wig!

Big pig wig.

IN, OUT, DOWN, UP
A Four-Word Story

In.

Out.

Down.

Up.

Up.

Down.

Down.

Up.

A Five-Word Story

Jake.

Jake bakes.

Jake bakes cake.

Snake.

Snake takes.

Snake takes cake.

JOANNA COLE

is the author of the best-selling Magic School Bus books as well as many other award-winning books, including *How You Were Born, Doctor Change, Anna Banana,* and *Riding Silver Star.*

STEPHANIE CALMENSON

has written many popular books for children, including *The Principal's New Clothes, It Begins with an A,* and *Dinner at the Panda Palace,* which was featured on PBS's "StoryTime."

TOGETHER

Joanna Cole and Stephanie Calmenson have created numerous books, including *Six Sick Sheep: 101 Tongue Twisters, Why Did the Chicken Cross the Road? And Other Riddles Old and New, Yours Till Banana Splits: 201 Autograph Rhymes, Ready...Set...Read!, Ready...Set...Read—and Laugh!, The Gator Girls,* and *The Gator Girls: Rockin' Reptiles.*

The authors have been Reading Bugs for as long as they can remember.

Are <u>you</u> a Reading Bug, too?